Central America

WELCOME TO OUR WORLD

Dedicated to

Grandpa and Grandma Budensiek
who first introduced our family to mission life.

Don and Devonna Moore whose quiet and godly lives have influenced and impacted more people than we will ever know.

© Copyright 2019   *Welcome to My World*
"By the Way" Series, Book 1
Central America

Author   Joy Budensiek
Cover   Mark Going
Editors   Julie Thompson, Faith Tofte, Louise Whitehead

ISBN   978-1-5323-9336-5

Photo Credits

Bigstock.com- photogallet1976, Mondik, mathes, Dudarev Mikhail, searagen, lucky12, Bernardo Ertl, Lucy Brown-loca4motion, zia_shusha, Eivaisla, Jorge Gonzalez, loeskieboom, vladispas, Seu Melhor Click, James Abroad, Imseco, StrangeView, THPStock, Kevin Wells Photography, ABV, phototrip, Nick Dale, rechitansorin, master1305, brizardh, holbox, Denise Campbell, kikkerdirk, fblanco7305, Pattamod, Rost-9, titoOnz, jevgenijkirilenko, Lew Marcrum, sigalavaca, Pachamedias, PixieMe, Yuriy Mayboroda, reisegraf.ch, Gearstd, rj lerich, Nikelser, Candyman, chrisimages, Taboga, mihmihmal, reisegraf.ch, fotosebek, Nachosuch, pattie, Edit One International, Gualberto107, Valleyboi63, dani3315, loeskieboom, phototrip, suns_luck, GraphicasRF, Gustavo Frazao, JosephCG, panuruangjan, twindesigner, Lawkeeper, George Vieira Silva, Loraliu, reisegraf.ch, mari_art.

Evangelistic Faith Missions, Steve Hight, Daniel Melton, Crystal Schaper, J Steven Manley; Florida Evangelistic Association, Benjamin McDowell, John Dykes, Glen Reiff; Evangelical Wesleyan Missions, Raymond Shreve, Hugh Wade Jr; Fundacion Emmanuel, Miriam Ceberia; Nazarene Missions, Roger Kellogg; Peace Evangelical Association, Lynan Redman; Spanish World Missions, Mary Duren; Touching Lives for Christ; True Gospel Mission, Tom Peak; Wesleyan Missions, Lydia Hines, Clara West. Rick Cessna, Chuck Holton. Katie Thompson. Pixabay-Multiple images.

RENEWANATION
PO Box 12366
Roanoke, VA 24025
1-855-TO-RENEW
info@renewanation.org

BY THE WAY BOOKS
PO Box 1065
Hobe Sound, FL 33475
joybudensiek@aol.com
bythewayseries.com

Information taken from *Operation World, 7th Edition,* Jason Mandruk, 2010, Biblica Publishing, Colorado Springs, CO.

All rights reserved. With the exception of quoting brief passages for purposes of review, no part of this publication, including photography, may be reproduced without prior and expressed written permission from the author.

Information in this book is true and complete to the best of the author's knowledge.
Scriptures: King James Version, Author's paraphrase.
Printed in the United States of America. M&K Publishing, Stuart, FL 34997.

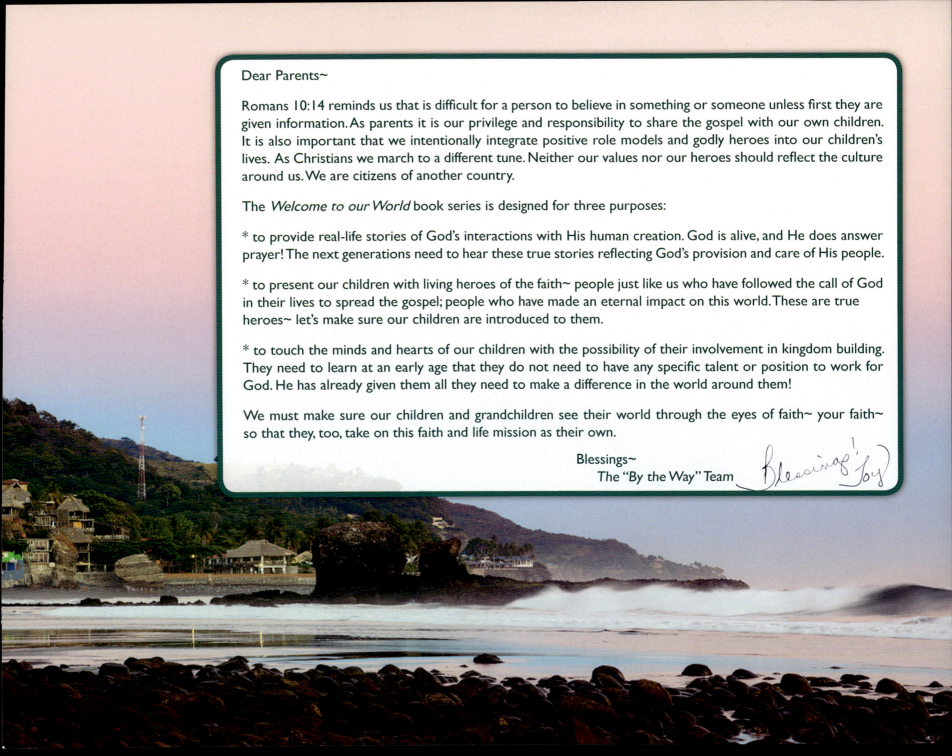

Dear Parents~

Romans 10:14 reminds us that is difficult for a person to believe in something or someone unless first they are given information. As parents it is our privilege and responsibility to share the gospel with our own children. It is also important that we intentionally integrate positive role models and godly heroes into our children's lives. As Christians we march to a different tune. Neither our values nor our heroes should reflect the culture around us. We are citizens of another country.

The *Welcome to our World* book series is designed for three purposes:

* to provide real-life stories of God's interactions with His human creation. God is alive, and He does answer prayer! The next generations need to hear these true stories reflecting God's provision and care of His people.

* to present our children with living heroes of the faith~ people just like us who have followed the call of God in their lives to spread the gospel; people who have made an eternal impact on this world. These are true heroes~ let's make sure our children are introduced to them.

* to touch the minds and hearts of our children with the possibility of their involvement in kingdom building. They need to learn at an early age that they do not need to have any specific talent or position to work for God. He has already given them all they need to make a difference in the world around them!

We must make sure our children and grandchildren see their world through the eyes of faith~ your faith~ so that they, too, take on this faith and life mission as their own.

Blessings~
The "By the Way" Team

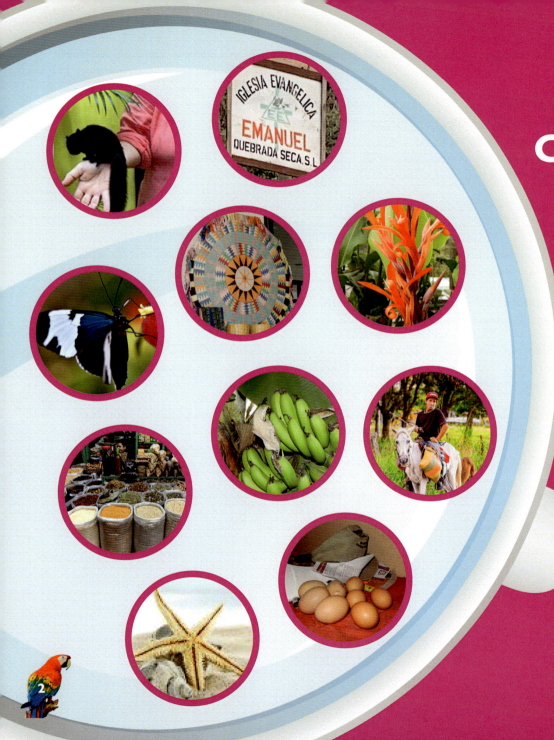

Come on, Kids~ Let's have some fun!

Try YOUR sleuthing skills as you read through the book.

See how many of these animals and objects you can find!

Buenos dias!
Welcome to our World!

"Uncle Francisco, what are you studying today?" asked Maria as she and her brother Juan came up the walk and sat on one of the comfortable chairs on their uncle's porch.

"History," replied Francisco. "I know we live here in Central America, but it's hard to wrap my mind around all the things which happened here over the many centuries."

"Did you know Central America was settled before the time of Christ?

"The people who settled here were Amerindians who crossed the land bridge that used to be between Asia and Alaska. Just like today, there are many, many individual nations~ each having their own language, customs, culture, religions and folklore."

"That's fascinating," said Juan. "I still have a hard time thinking about HUGE civilizations completely disappearing, and all we have left today are some pretty impressive ruins."

"Oh, but we have something else," said Uncle Francisco.

"What's that?" asked Maria.

"Stories~ lots of stories. Both from long ago and even today. How about you discovering some stories about our part of the world?"

"That sounds challenging," said Juan, "but I'm up to it. How about you, Maria?"

"Sure," Maria replied. "I always like a good challenge.

"Let's not go find just any kind of stories~ let's find **missionary stories from our own Central America."**

"Well, that sounds like an even better plan," said Uncle Francisco. "Come on and join us!"

Central America

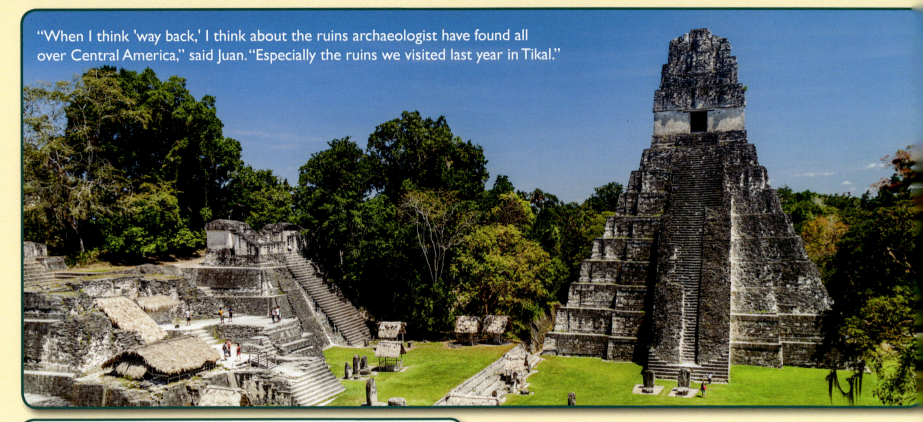

"When I think 'way back,' I think about the ruins archaeologist have found all over Central America," said Juan. "Especially the ruins we visited last year in Tikal."

Did you know? Early Mayans~

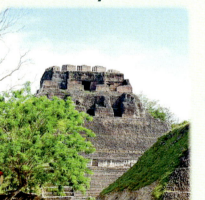

loved chocolate.

wrote books.

used 0 as a symbol for nothing.

filed their teeth into sharp points if they were noble women.

were excellent bee keepers.

used astronomy and math to devise calendars.

Uncle Francisco said, "While there were Indian civilizations all throughout Central America, the 'Old World' across the Atlantic Ocean had begun a new era of exploration. Men like Vasco de Gama, Christopher Columbus, de las Casas and Magellan began to sail west looking for gold and riches. They also took the Catholic faith wherever they went.

"Christopher Columbus came ashore in Honduras and Nicaragua. These explorers were not always kind to the Amerindians they found. In fact sometimes at the point of a sword they forced the Indians to accept the Christian faith. The native people however were not giving up all of their pagan faiths~ they simply accepted parts of the Catholic faith and came up with a new s 'Christianity.'"

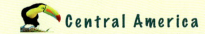
Central America

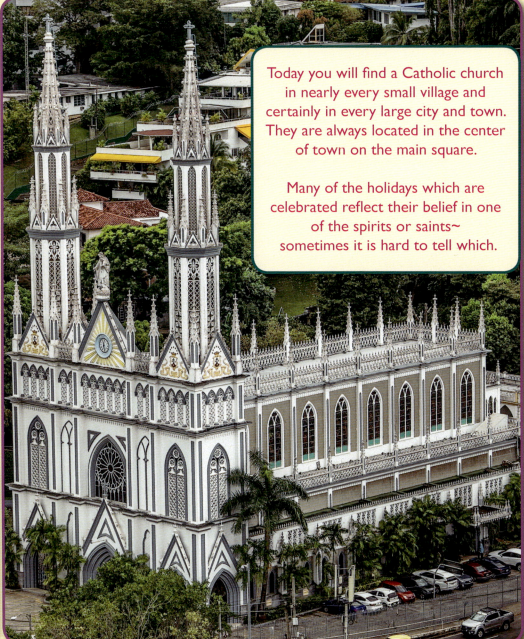

Today you will find a Catholic church in nearly every small village and certainly in every large city and town. They are always located in the center of town on the main square.

Many of the holidays which are celebrated reflect their belief in one of the spirits or saints~ sometimes it is hard to tell which.

Central America

For many years the blend of Catholicism and paganism in Central America was the religion of the people. Across the Atlantic Ocean Martin Luther posted his 95 theses on the door of the Wittenburg church.

Strong men of God began to understand and realize salvation comes through faith in Christ and not by works or traditions.

Along with that knowledge God began to speak to the early Protestant missionaries about "going into all the world to preach the gospel." Many thousands responded. In those early days the missionaries usually went to faraway places like India, China or the "Dark Continent" of Africa. No one seemed to think very much about the lost who lived closer to home.

"What about Samaria?"

But God had not forgotten. Down in Costa Rica the wives of two ranchers faithfully prayed that God would send a missionary to them~ to their country and their part of the world.

Sometimes God uses the most unlikely people to fulfill His purpose. A lawyer, C. I. Scofield, was enjoying his life of sin, especially drinking. Through the faithful witness of one of his clients, he heard about Jesus and was genuinely converted. His life totally changed!

He became interested in Bible study and prayer. One day while praying for the missionaries, he realized he was praying for the "uttermost parts of the world." All of a sudden he stopped short. What did God mean when He referred to "Samaria"? No one he was acquainted with had thought about the lost in "Samaria." Could that be Central America? It was.

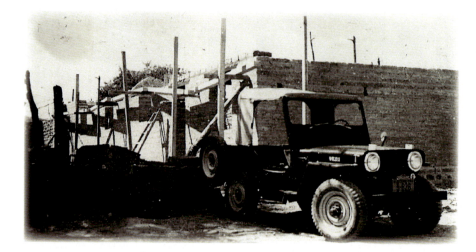

Now God was going to answer the prayers of the two ladies. People were ready to hear the good news of the gospel. In just a few short years, hundreds of missionaries would go into all seven Central American countries and spread the good news and build many churches in their own "Samaria."

Central America

New churches sprang up all over Central America.

Whole families heard the gospel and turned to Jesus.

Guatemala's First Evangelical Martyr

Sometimes sharing the gospel comes at a high price~ the price of a life.

Max Vasquez felt the call of God on his life. He and his wife went to Alotenango, a Mayan village at the foot of one of Guatemala's active volcanoes. Here he faithfully preached with love and compassion. Many, including drunkards, thieves and murderers found new life in Christ. Many new believers were converted, and the church was growing.

But not everyone was happy about this. The Catholic priest and some of the local officials were mad. They stirred up the villagers to attack the church and pastor. It was Holy Week 1953 that a mob stormed the church. With their sharp machetes, they whacked up everything in sight, then turned on Max and his family. His family, though injured, were able to escape. Max was not so fortunate.

The cruel mob beat and stoned Max until he died. Hundreds from all over Guatemala attended his funeral. But his story didn't end there. Several of his attackers, after sobering up, realized what they had done. They began attending church and got saved. They went on to further spread the gospel.

It was during Max's funeral as a plea went out for others to take Max's place that a 17-year-old boy stepped forward, dedicating his life for missionary service.

We know him today as our beloved friend and missionary statesman, Dr. Glen Reiff.

Central America

CRISTO ME AMA

(Jesus Loves Me)

Cristo me ama, bien lo se
Su palabra dice así;
Que los niños son de aquel;
Quien es nuestro amigo fiel.
Si, Cristo me ama,
Si, Cristo me ama,
Si, Cristo me ama,
La Biblia dice asi.

Central America

The Peoples of Central America

Most of the people of Central America are from mixed ancestry.
Eighty two percent are a mixture of European and Americans.
They are called "mestizos."
Twelve percent are from only European backgrounds.
Five percent descended from European and African ancestors.
They are called "mulattoes."
One percent are Amerindians and black.

Who we are and where we come from makes no difference.
Jesus loves all the children of the world~
red and yellow, black and white~ or whatever the mixture.
He loves ALL of us exactly the same.

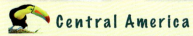

Central America

Water Win! Win!
Roger and Damaris Kellogg

How would you like to drink from a mud puddle? For many people in Central America collecting water from huge mud puddles or a thatched roof during the rainy season will be their only water supply for the remainder of the year. Many people die due to waterborne illnesses.

What a huge blessing it was to Los Cerritos, Peten (12 hours north of Guatemala City) when God provided funds for the community to have their own 1500-gallon plastic water container.

This water is definitely cleaner than the mud puddles! Those same funds helped many families replace their thatched roofs with tin roofs. Special clay water filters were also provided to each family to filter their drinking and cooking water.

Mud puddles may be fun to play in but NOT for drinking!
Today the community is not only enjoying clean drinking water,
but many have also come to Christ, the source of our living water!

Don't Step! It's a Coral Snake!
Mrs. Lynan Redman

We had long ago left the security of our faithful jeep and were now "hiking" through overgrown jungle to hold an open-air meeting in a remote Guatemalan village.

National friends were carrying benches and my mom's accordion. My dad had his trusty Bible and lantern. People would come from all over the mountains to hear what the "gringos" had to share.

All of a sudden the national walking beside my mother put out his arm, stopping her from taking the next step. He pointed down. There was a deadly coral snake leisurely slithering its way across the path at EXACTLY the point my mother would have stepped. Had she stepped on the snake, she almost certainly would have been bitten and death would have quickly followed.

That was close! Thank God for His protection. Later my grandmother asked my mother, "Have you recently been in danger?"

Thinking back, my mother replied, "Yes, I almost stepped on a coral snake."

When they compared times, they discovered God had given my grandmother an urgency to pray at exactly the same time my mother was walking down the path. Thousands of miles apart~ but both near to the heart of God.

God does hear AND answers prayer!

Central America

Feliz Navidad, Feliz Navidad~
We wish you a merry Christmas!

Today was the day their friend and missionary Juan Gomez and his family were coming to their village. He came often, but today was special! Today they would be celebrating the birth of Christ. Afterward Pastor Juan would be passing out their Christmas treats!

They had not always known about Jesus. It was not many years ago that God called an older man, Don Speicher, who was entering retirement to hitch up a little old trailer, drive through Mexico and eventually find his way to Mam territory. Mr. Speicher could not speak the language, but God brought three teenage boys to him, and he taught them English!

He loved "his people," and they knew it! If there was a birth, a death, a celebration of any kind~ Mr. Speicher was there! There was nothing he enjoyed more than baptismal services. How happy he was to know so many were finding Jesus as their Savior.

Churches began to spring up all through Mam territory. After several years one of his adopted boys, Juan, became the leader. Just like Mr. Speicher, his heart beat with love for his people.

Pastor Juan worked hard to make sure every family received their Christmas gift. People had been generous, and donations were good. This year every family would receive a large bag of sugar, coffee, rice, a chicken, and of course candy for the children!

Oh, yes, don't forget the firecrackers.

No celebration in Guatemala would be complete without fireworks!

This Christmas there was much to celebrate! The gospel had come to their village, and they knew the true meaning of Christmas!

Central America

WELCOME TO Guatemala
"Land of Eternal Springtime"

The Quetzal bird is Guatemala's national bird, symbolizing freedom.

Its body is only 5-6 inches, but the tail is a beautiful 21 inches.

You will not find this bird in a zoo~ only glimpses of it in the wild. If captured, it will commit suicide.

Its nest has a front and back door with the bird entering from the back. It cannot back up. Its feathers would be injured, and it would die.

Guatemala has at least 37 volcanoes.

Three volcanoes are currently active~ Pacaya, Fuego, and Santiaguito.

Yeah! Soccer

Beauty and flowers are an important part of Guatemalan life. However, be careful not to give white flowers~ those are only given when someone dies.

From 1960 through 1996 Guatemala suffered a horrible civil war. Many people were killed, whole villages fled in terror, and everyone suffered terribly. In 1996 a Peace Accord was signed. Since then every day at 11:30, a fresh white rose is placed by an Army Honor Guard on a monument in the palace courtyard.

Guatemala is known for its colorful textiles.

Blue denim was invented here.

There are 11 Mayan mountain groups. Each group has its own distinctive clothing.

Guatemala is the world's largest producer of jade.

Guatemala has the perfect weather and altitude for raising coffee. For many years Guatemala was the number one coffee producer in all of Central America.

God's Helicopter
Mrs. Miriam Cebeira

Surely the horror stories of starving people of the Ixil territories of northern Guatemala had been exaggerated~ but no, they were pathetically and heartbreakingly real. During Guatemala's civil war many villagers were caught between loyalty to the government and Communist guerrillas. Whole villages had been burned.

The only possible solution the people had was to flee high up into the mountains. There, many of them lived for 12 years, eating only wild herbs and roots and sleeping in tree-branch shelters. It is estimated 200,000 died. When the war ended, people began trickling down from the mountains. They were starving, diseased and absolutely destitute.

> His light is shining brightly in these mountains and jungles of those who are "back home!"

Many trips by foot and donkey were made to bring relief to these precious people. Then God provided a helicopter to reach villages that could never have been reached otherwise. In Jesus' name medicine, food bags, free fruit trees, animals and candy were freely given. Today, pastors ride motorcycles to remote villages every week sharing the gospel.

God has blessed these "forgotten people" with more than 185 churches, 6 radio stations, and 12 Bible schools through the ministry of Fundacion Emmanuel.

Snap, Crackle, Pop, Fire!
Mrs. Miriam Cebeira

The loudspeaker system snapped, crackled, popped and then flames shot out. The missionaries looked at each other~ what should they do? They had come to this remote village knowing they were NOT wanted, and could even possibly be killed. Now, under the night sky in the open-air service it seem the forces of Satan were incredibly strong~ even t loudspeaker system had rebelled.

The faithful national pastors and missionaries pray They committed everything, including their lives, to God then laid down and went to sleep. The angels of the Lord truly encamped around about them th night. The next morning, just out of curiosity, they started up the generator and plugged in the loudspeaker system.

> It worked perfectly!

Satan's power had been defeated. They continued to hold services and before the weekend was over 26 people had bravely stepped forward to become believers in Jesus!

> After all, if He could bring a burning loudspeaker system back to life, surely HE could bring hope and peace into their pain-filled lives!

Guatemala

How Can a Saint Be Made of Wood?
Mrs. Mary Duren

Raul inched closer to get a better look. He could not believe his eyes~ surely something was wrong. There right in front of him the Catholic church fathers were dressing one of the saints. When they took the old clothes off, Raul could see all sorts of boards, hinges and screws holding the saint together. He was only a little guy~ seven years old, but this did not make sense.

How could something made with boards and screws answer his prayers?

Up until now, he had faithfully prayed to the saints~ but now he was not so sure.

Several years later Raul was a successful businessman. So successful that people KNEW what was in his briefcase~ MONEY and lots of it. One day while walking on a sidewalk in Guatemala City, a robber fired his gun. Raul's spinal cord was hit which immediately paralyzed him. His money, health, future and hope was all gone in a split second.

Desperate to pray~ but still not sure about the saint's ability to answer, Raul prayed, "God, if there really is a God, please send someone to me."

God, the Master planner, already had plans in motion for Brady and Mary Duren to start a church just three blocks from Raul's

home. Their original plan of returning to the coast just had not worked out. For no apparent reason their hearts were drawn to this part of town.

Shortly after arriving their friend Rev. Joe Smith came and preached a revival in their new church. Raul was there and prayed to the true God who is not made of wood and gadgets. He prayed to the God who really does hear AND answer prayer.

Raul later became the pastor of the church. Brady and Mary continue their faithful ministry of love to thousands of Guatemalans and Hondurans~ both in the city and mountain villages. Brady's gift of "helps" Mary's gift of "happiness" has blessed thousands.

There is great religious freedom in Guatemala.

Twenty-four percent of the people are evangelicals.

The Catholic Church is declining in influence.

Crusades, Christian schools, magazines, and personal witness are all being used in widespread evangelism.

National believers are involved in Bible translation.

"Why Doesn't Your God Speak My Language?"

Cameron listened as the representative from the Bible House of Los Angeles appealed for Bible salesmen to go to Latin America and sell Bibles for the summer. That sounded like something he could do~ why not?

He and his friend were assigned to Guatemala. And now, here he was high up in the mountains of Guatemala trying to sell Spanish Bibles to these proud Mayan descendants. He loved being here, but there was one huge problem. He could not speak their language, and they certainly could not speak English. It did help to speak in Spanish, but Cam knew this was not their "mother tongue."

His world was shaken when a Cakhiquel Indian lady asked him~

"Why, if you God is so smart, hasn't he learned our language?" It was a simple question, but it changed Cameron's life forever.

Through that question Cameron heard God's call to translate the Bible into the Cakchiquel language. It took ten long years to complete the first translation. In the meantime he shared his vision of translating the Bible into the "heart languages" for ALL of the 6,000 Bible-less peoples of the world.

His vision caught on, and Wycliffe Bible Translators was born. For over 75 years missionaries have been going all over the world to translate the Bible into minority language groups. Often life in general improves for these tribal people. Cameron Townsend became recognized as a world linguistic and translation pioneer. His work took him from the poorest and humblest dwellings into the palaces of kings and national presidents.

Jesus, My Very Best Friend

Many years after Uncle Cam translated the scriptures in the Cakhiquel language, another little book, *Jesus, My Very Best Friend,* was translated from English into Spanish and then into the Mam language.

Short-term mission teams would take the little book to many Mam villages. Not only children, but often older people gladly received the message that Jesus truly is their best friend.

"The greatest missionary is the Bible in the mother tongue. It needs no furlough and is never considered a foreigner."
Uncle Cam Townsend

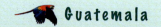

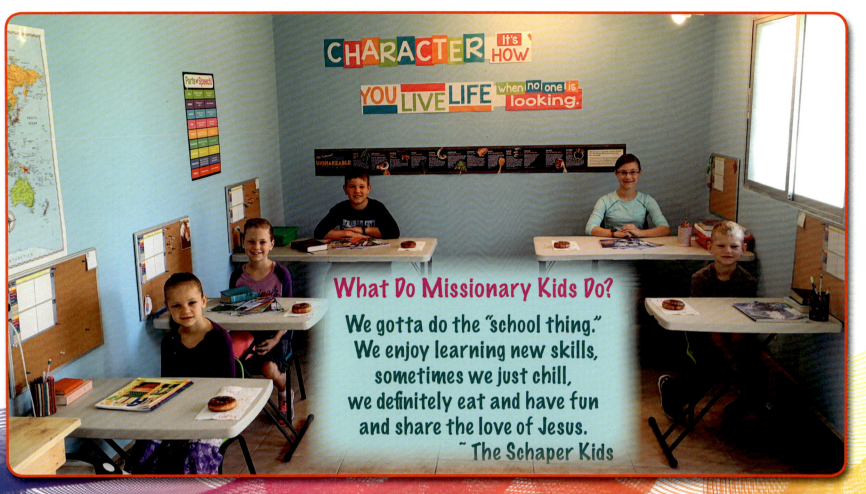

What Do Missionary Kids Do?

We gotta do the "school thing."
We enjoy learning new skills,
sometimes we just chill,
we definitely eat and have fun
and share the love of Jesus.
~ The Schaper Kids

Kristyn

Owen

Ashlyn

Jeren

Megan

Guatemala

Belize
"Jewel in the Heart of the Caribbean Basin"

Cricket ~ The official Belizian Sport

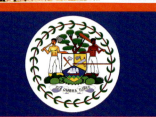

Belize is the only country to have people represented on their flag.

Belize is home to the only jaguar reserve in the world.

The jabiru stork found in Belize is the largest flying bird in the Americas.

Eighty percent of Belize is rain forest. Over 500 species of orchids live here.

Their phrase "canopy of forest" means "Under the Shade I Flourish."

Howler monkeys are among the ten loudest animals in the world.

English is the official language of Belize.

Ambergris Caye was the long ago hideout of pirate ships which attacked the Spanish fleet.

Belize is the only Central American country that does not border the Pacific Ocean.

Death Trap on the River
Rev. Hugh Wade

It was December 31, 1986, and the rainy season had come in all of its fury. Roads were impassable, and the only way to travel was by boat. That was not necessarily a problem. There was not anything unusual about boat travel in Belize.

That night around 10:30 p.m. Rev. Wade got in his boat to travel downstream about a mile to pick up people for their annual watch-night service. He checked the engine, pulled the cord, and off he went. Everything seemed to be in perfect order until he got about 100 feet from the dock and the engine died. This happened three times! What was going on?

Rev. Wade prayed, "God, if you don't want me to go downriver, please help the engine start, and I'll turn around and go back home." The engine immediately cranked up. He turned the boat and headed home~ assuming that for some reason it seemed God did not want him going down the river.

That watch-night service had been extraordinarily blessed by the presence of God. There were new converts~ it had been a wonderful night. At the end of the service, one of his faithful friends came up to him and asked, "Brother 'Huge,' why didn't you come pick us up tonight? Did you have engine problems?"

Pastor Wade responded, "Well, yes and no," telling the strange story.

His friend then told him what he had discovered. "What you didn't know was, someone who is very angry with you wanted to kill you tonight. A wire was strung across the river. You would not have seen it, but going normal speed, it would have killed you.

"Angels watched out for you tonight.

"Not only was your life spared but God gave us a wonderful watch-night service." He truly does watch out for His own! Several years later the man became a Christian AND a good friend.

Evangelicals have had steady growth.
Most Belizeans profess Christianity.
Belize is a secular state with religious freedom.
The Bible is a public school required textbook from elementary to university level.
Only 10% of the population regularly attend church.

"Where He leads, I'll follow, and what He feeds, I'll swallow."

The Flying Fish and Lost Letter
Rev. Hugh Wade

"YOU ARE CRAZY! Do you mean to tell me you're leaving a good paying government job and going out to pastor a little church that can't pay you a cent?" asked my very upset father.

"Yes, I believe that is what God is calling me to do," I replied. But if I could have known just how hard it was going to be, I may not have sounded so definite.

A few months later rainy season had come, which meant the riverbanks had overflowed. You cannot catch fish in flooded conditions. We had nearly eaten everything we had~ the cupboards were empty, and it was only mid-month. As my wife and I sat thinking about our situation, I asked her, "If you could have anything in the world to eat, what would it be?"

She thought for a moment and then said, "I'd sure like a nice big piece of fish." That was wishful thinking to be sure!

That night when I went by boat to pick up some of our church people for church, I felt my propeller hit something. The next thing I knew, a BIG fish flew through the air and landed on the bank. Instead of slipping back into the water, it flopped to higher ground. What a supper we had that night~ exactly what my wife wanted. The very next day the postman sheepishly asked me my name. I told him it was "Hugh."

"Oh," he said, "I always thought you had the same name as your father~ Walter. I've had a letter at the post office for three weeks addressed to 'Hugh' but didn't know who to give it to."

God spoke to a little congregation in Michigan that His servants in Belize needed some money. They took up an offering which amounted to $250. Every single month thereafter a check for $250 promptly arrived from them until God called us to another pastorate which could pay my salary.

EL SALVADOR
"Land of Volcanoes"

As the smallest country in the continental Americas El Salvador is called the "Tom Thumb of the Americas."

Soccer is the "flaming favorite" sport in El Salvador.

El Salvadorians call themselves "guanacos."

"El Salvador" actually means "Republic of the Savior."

Coffee is El Salvador's biggest export.

If invited to dinner, always go 30-45 minutes late~ otherwise you are considered rude.

Salvadorian women greet each other by patting arms.

El Salvador is the only Central American country without a Caribbean coastline.

There are 20 active volcanoes in El Salvador.

El Salvador has two seasons~ rainy season is from May to October, dry season from November to June.

El Imposible is El Salvador's largest national park.
It has over 800 species of orchids,
1,000 species of butterflies,
500 species of birds,
400 species of orchids,
800 species of trees,
and 800
marine fish.

23

The 100-Hour Soccer War

Diego sighed. His country of El Salvador had just gone to war AGAIN. It seemed like for as long as he could remember his family had talked about one war or another. Now it was 1969, and their soccer team had a fantastic year~ in fact, they were headed to the three-match World Soccer Cup! Their opponent? Honduras.

The two countries had become bitter rivals, not only on the soccer field but also in business ventures, migrant situations and land disputes. Now, all the pent-up frustration and anger had played out on the soccer field.

After the first two games, rioting had broken out. That was the last straw. War was declared. Anger and national pride on both sides flares. Troops marched, and planes flew overhead dropping bombs.

Leaders from all over Central America quickly met to resolve the situation. After 100 hours a shaky peace treaty was signed but only after over 2,000 lives had been lost. Juan knew life would go on, but it sure would be easier if they had Jesus in their hearts.

Headlights Under Water
Dr. Glen Reiff

Our family had been ministering in the country of El Salvador when the call came from one of the churches that we needed to go conduct a funeral. The church was several hours away. The trip had gone fine until just a few miles from the church we had to cross a stream. Normally, that would not be a big deal. Today it was! The waters had swollen past the banks and the current was obviously very strong.

Gritting my teeth, I drove into the water. A few seconds later I was safely on the other side. But there stood a family on the bank desperate to get across~ would I please help them? Breathing a quick prayer, I said, "Yes." Once again, we made it safely across in good time. BUT I had to once again return through the water. By now the water was much higher and the current much faster.

Adrenaline shot through my body. I gripped the steering wheel and for the third time entered the swirling river. This time water quickly rose, covered the lights and splashed onto the hood. It was pitch black. There was no human way across the water. Just as I was nearing desperation, I felt the tires grab onto something~ it was the river bank! God had directed my steering and brought me safely across!

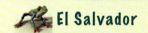 El Salvador

"Hey, Man, It's Me, Gustavo!"
Mrs. Lydia Hines

Gustavo was a drug addict and an alcoholic. He was only 15, and already his bad habits were eating up his money. He spent time in jail for stealing.

One day Gustavo met Pastor Alejandro who led him to Jesus. Jesus changed everything. Gustavo gladly began helping in the church. But when Pastor Alejandro suggested they go preach in Gustavo's old barrio (neighborhood), Gustavo did not want to go.

"Not there," he said. "Everybody over there knows what a bad person I have been."

But the pastor kept insisting, and finally Gustavo agreed. When his former neighbors found out Gustavo was preaching, they came to hear him. They were curious to know what had happened to him!

Every faith has freedom of religion. Thirty percent of El Salvadorians live outside the country. Many others moved from the country to the city resulting in increased poverty and crime.
In 1960 2% of the population were evangelicals. By 2010 that number had jumped to 32%.

It was not an easy place to plant a church. Three times when Gustavo was walking to church, he was robbed. One night right out in front of the church, a guy grabbed him, pointed a gun at him, and threatened to kill him if he didn't give him money. Gustavo recognized the man from his days of living on the street. "Hey, man he said. "It's me, Gustavo!"

"Oh, sorry! I didn't know it was you," the guy said.

Gustavo got him calmed down and later began studying the Bible with him and helping him get his life straightened out. Other people in the barrio also came to Jesus. What a difference He made in their lives! Instead of going after drugs, Gustavo and his wife are now going after people and bringing them to Jesus.

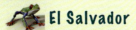
El Salvador

Honduras
"Great Depths"

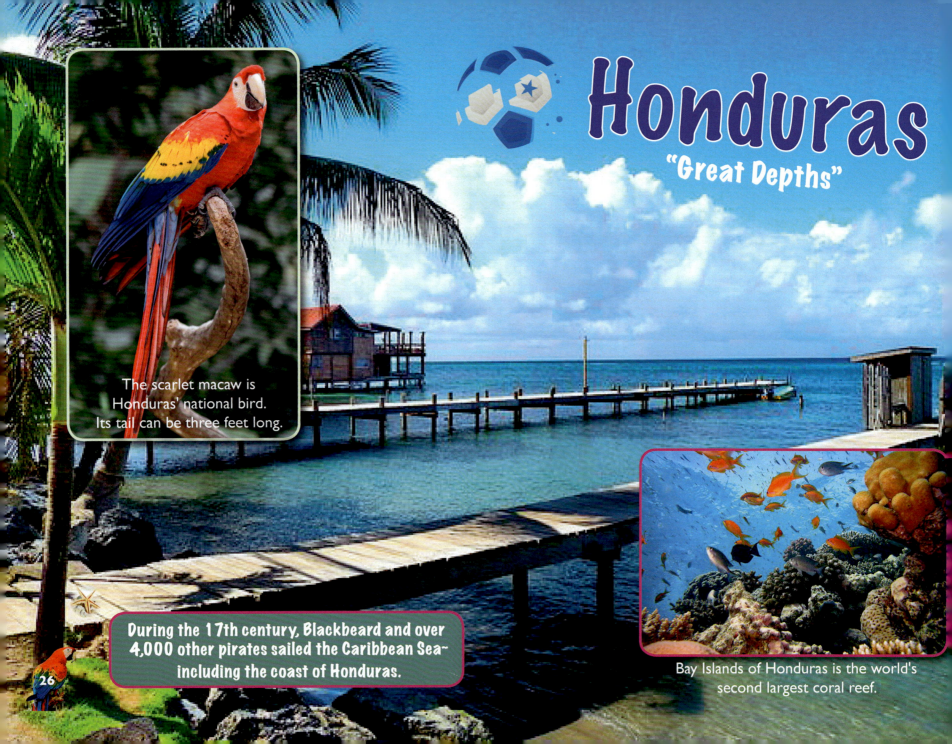

The scarlet macaw is Honduras' national bird. Its tail can be three feet long.

During the 17th century, Blackbeard and over 4,000 other pirates sailed the Caribbean Sea~ including the coast of Honduras.

Bay Islands of Honduras is the world's second largest coral reef.

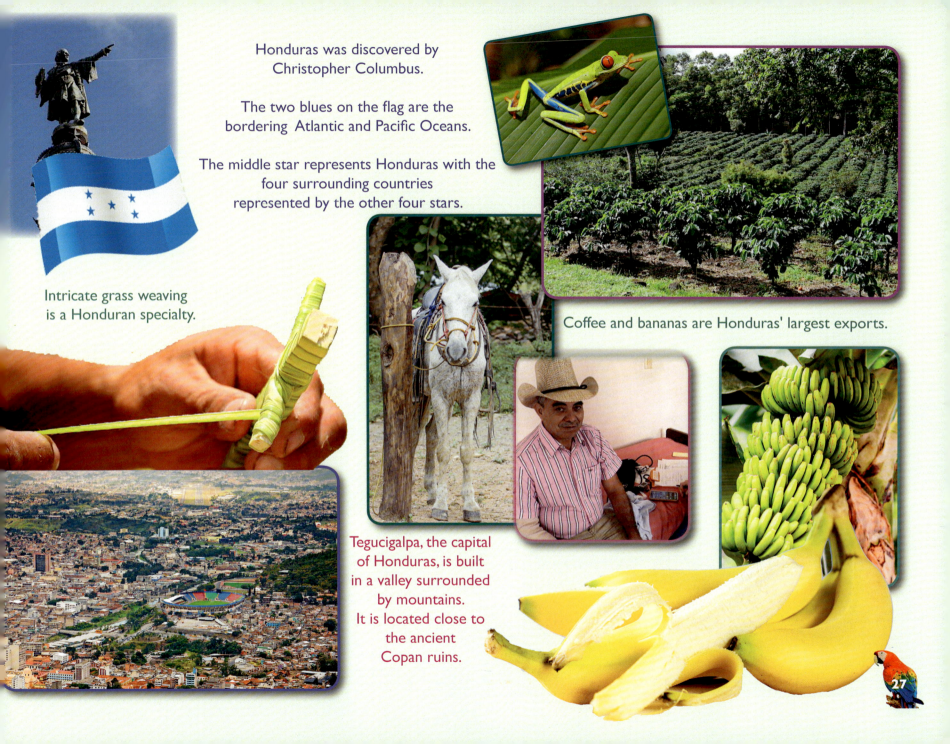

Honduras was discovered by Christopher Columbus.

The two blues on the flag are the bordering Atlantic and Pacific Oceans.

The middle star represents Honduras with the four surrounding countries represented by the other four stars.

Intricate grass weaving is a Honduran specialty.

Coffee and bananas are Honduras' largest exports.

Tegucigalpa, the capital of Honduras, is built in a valley surrounded by mountains. It is located close to the ancient Copan ruins.

"Hang On, We're Going Through"

The night air was getting cooler as the jeep climbed up the mountain road. Not long ago the sun had set, and now it was dark~ very, very dark. Little houses stood along the road with lights from a fire filtering through the adobe cracks. The missionary family and their American friends had been in San Pedro Sula for the day and were returning home.

What an exciting day it had been. Earlier that morning a helicopter had landed on the little airstrip at San Luis. What a pleasant and unexpected surprise to have eight American military guys get off the plane! This was just a stopover for them. Their mission was to go higher into the mountains taking medical help to the mountain people. Of course they enjoyed touring the mission clinic

while at San Luis. As the Americans flew away, one of the guests said, "Well, I wonder what tonight holds. This morning we were visited by the American military~ good guys. Maybe tonight we'll see some bad guys." Needless to say, that statement was not very appreciated. For sure no one wanted those words to come true!

After the Americans left, the Moore's and their friends drove the forty miles up and over the mountain road to finally arrive in

Honduras

...n Pedro Sula. Getting groceries, gathering supplies for the clinic ...d radio station and lots of other stops all took longer than expected. It was getting later in the day~ with a mountain drive still ...ead of them when the missionary said, "I just can't come to town ...thout getting my usual ice cream cone."

...nd so they all sat down to enjoy a delicious ice cream cone. ...while later with full tummies they started home. Everyone was in ... happy and jolly mood until the pavement stopped and became a ...rrow dirt road. The quietness and darkness settled in.

Everything went fine for a while. Then right in front of the jeep was a group of ten men with the headlights bouncing off their machetes.
This was for real. Here they were, high on a Honduras mountain, no one around, in absolute darkness with the road blocked!
Quick and desperate prayers rose to heaven.

"Dear Jesus, please help us. You see the danger we are in." Don, the ...river quickly looked at the situation and announced, "Hang on! ...e're going through." He put the pedal down and miraculously the ...roup divided in two~ half to the right, half to the left. The mission...ry and his friends went right through the middle.

...ut the back window the men could be seen chasing the jeep ...p the road, but not for long. It is not hard to imagine God dispatched two angels that night to keep His children safe. I could imagine those two angels ~ one on each side of the road holding out their arms, keeping the "bad guys" back and allowing God's servants to pass by unharmed.

More than half of Honduras' population is children. There are thousands of "street children" with nowhere to live.

While the Roman Catholic Church is the "official religion," everyone has religious freedom.

The devastation of Hurricane Mitch has left most of the country below poverty level.

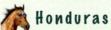

Honduras

Saved in the Engine Room
Rev. Sid Grant

"Sid, you've got to learn how to swim. You have nearly drowned twice in your short life; we can't take any more chances!" said his frightened mother. And she was right! Sid, his parents and 13 other

siblings lived on an island with water all around. Most days the ocean was like a gigantic playground~ fishing for conch, deep water diving and eventually swimming were all part of his childhood. On Sundays Mom sent her children to church, but Sid had no time to think about God. His mind was on other things and his exciting future.

He dreamed of going to America, making money and getting some education. Eventually he wanted to return to Honduras, get married, have children and build a house. He had it all figured out! And life did seem to go his way~ at least for a while. At 19 his father helped him get a job on an ocean liner based in West Palm Beach, Florida. His dreams were beginning to come true.

He was a true sailor~ sailing the ocean blue!

And then one day when the ship docked in Trinidad, he was given a telegram telling that his mother had passed away. Adding to his troubles, he found out his finance had broken off their engagement. Now nothing seemed quite right. All of a sudden life got empty. It did not help any that his buddy Sam Williams left on vacation.

"Sid," said Sam just before leaving, "I'm going on vacation, but here is a New Testament. You need to read it while I'm gone. Maybe this will help you." Surprisingly Sid did begin to read, and read, and read. He read it all the way from beginning to end. And through the scripture God talked to Sid. But life was becoming more and more miserable.

Around three o'clock one morning, as the *Inagua Sound* plowed through the Caribbean waters, Sid was on duty in the engine room. He was thinking about how miserable his life had become. In desperation Sid said, "God, if there is anything better in life than this, I want it. I'm tired of the way my life is now."

It seemed God instantly replied, "There is a better life. You can have it through believing on Jesus. You can have a brand new life in Me."

There alone in the engine room of an ocean liner, Sid gave his heart and life to God. Truly, everything changed! It did not take long for the other sailors to know something had happened. He was a new creation~ even the salty sailor language changed!

Within a year Sid had left the ship, began dating a Christian girl, gone back to school and received a call to preach the gospel.

God truly had given him the desires of his heart!

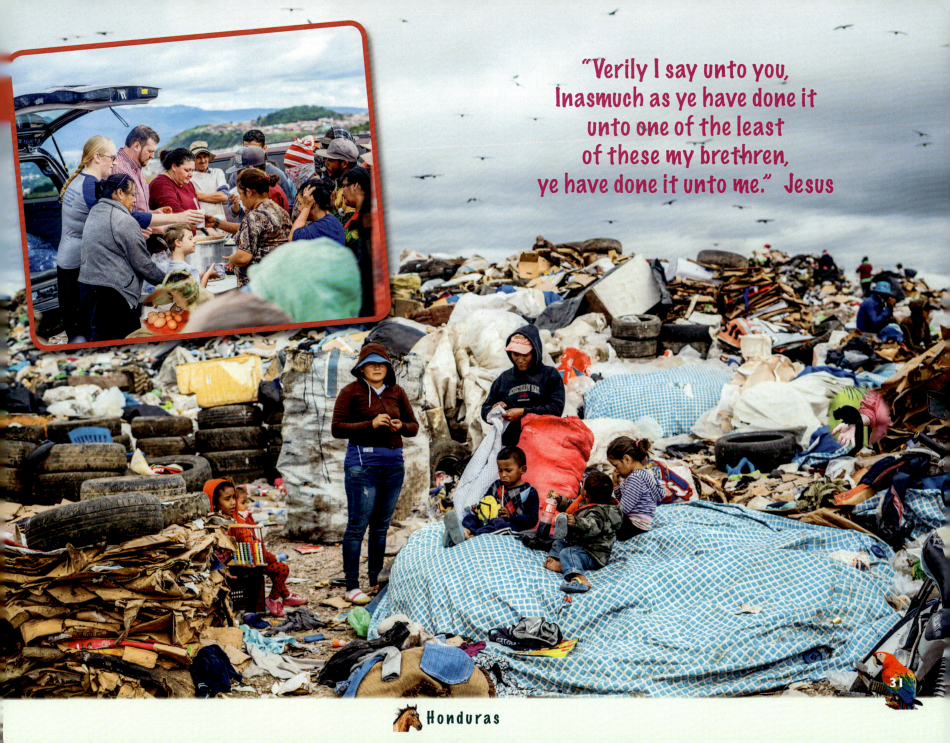

"Verily I say unto you, Inasmuch as ye have done it unto one of the least of these my brethren, ye have done it unto me." Jesus

Honduras

Many places in Nicaragua do not have street names. "Home" is wherever you hang your hat or hammock.

Baseball is a favorite Nicaraguan sport.

About 50 miles off the eastern coast of Nicaragua are two islands~ the Big and Little Corn Islands.

Nicaragua is the largest Central American country. Now that is something to crow about!

A favorite Nicaraguan breakfast food is called "Rooster." It consists of white rice and small red beans.

The poison dart frog, usually found near the ground, is very dangerous.

The brighter the frog~ the more toxic The frog got its name from some Amerindian tribes who use its poison to put on the end of their darts.

33

Building Up the Kingdom Wall

"Sh-h-h! Be quiet. Don't make any noise. I'm not sure who is close by, and I sure don't know if they are our friends." Quietly the host missionary of a short-term mission team stepped into the courtyard while the owner shut the door. "What do you want, and why are you here?" he asked.

"I have a team of 12 Americans with me, and we need a place to stay tonight," explained the host missionary.

"I'm so sorry, but I can't put my family in danger by allowing you to stay here," replied the home owner. "Just today, for the first time in many years, there was a group of Communist who came through our village. Besides that, we are a strongly Catholic community, and I'm quite sure they wouldn't want you to be here. The best I can offer you is my little cottage higher up in the mountains. I don't think anyone would bother you there."

With no other choice, the missionary and the group of Americans traveled on through the night. It was a scary ride. No one knew what or who lurked in the shadows. They finally made it to the cottage and slept fitfully that night. As daylight dawned, the team could see that the surrounding countryside was beautiful.

The project the team had come to complete was to build a new wall around the mission compound~ right in the middle of the village they could not stay last night. With a bit of fear and trembling, the team went back and began the hard task of tearing down the old wall and replacing it with a new one.

The day wore on with the bright sun shining down. It was obvious the team was not there to make trouble. They had a big, dirty, hard job to do. Around mid-afternoon the host missionary, who had bee in town, returned to the group. He called everyone together. "Kids, while I was in town the mayor contacted me. He said, 'We in the vi lage have been watching your team. They are good hard workers. W like their friendly smiles. We would be happy for you to stay in our town as long as you'd like.'"

What a change! For the next few days the team worked hard~ not only finishing the wall, but playing street soccer with the children, passing out literature and shopping at the local tiendas.

God's love literally broke down walls of fear, mistrust and hatred.

Before the team left, the leader was personally invited to the mayor's office where he expressed appreciation and asked for school supplies for needy children in his area. Later, teams were able to take hundreds of backpack and blankets to the families in his district.

Who would have ever thought that building a wall would break down so many barriers.

Truly God's ways are past our finding out!

Nicaragua

For Lack of Evidence
Rev. Raymond Shreve

Have you ever been hungry? Really, really hungry, and there was NO food? Luis Aguilera of Nicaragua knew what it was to be hungry~ really, really hungry! When he was four years old his mother died of a disease caused by being drunk too many times, and his father was later killed in a street fight. From then on he and his brother William lived in the back streets, alleys and garbage dumps of the cities of Nicaragua.

Most of the time the only way he could eat was to steal from street vendors. Sometimes he would find things he could eat that other people had thrown away. He never went to school but taught himself the alphabet and could sound out a few words.

At age 15 he was standing on a street corner when he saw a boy snatch a lady's purse, duck between the people, and run away. The lady began to scream, "Thief, thief!"

A policeman who was standing a few feet away turned around, grabbed Luis and asked the lady, "Is this the thief?"

The lady looked Luis up and down and finally said, "Yes, he is the one." The policeman drug Luis off to jail, telling the lady to be in court the next morning at 9:00 o'clock. That night, lying on the cold cement floor, Luis prayed his first prayer. He said, "God, if You are really there and will help, I promise You I will be good the rest of my life."

The next morning the policeman told the judge Luis stole the lady's purse, and the lady agreed. The judge then surprised everyone by asking two questions: "Did Luis have the purse?" And, "If he did it, why did he stay there and not run away?"

The judge dropped the charges "for lack of evidence." He also arranged for Luis to go to a boarding school where he learned to read and write. Then he was apprenticed to a baker who taught him the trade.

The first thing Luis did when he was released from jail was to find a church where he might thank God for helping him while he was in trouble. He went to the City Cathedral, but found it closed and locked. He went to another church and found it too closed. He found a statue of Christ in the churchyard and kneeling before it gave thanks for helping him and renewed his promise to be good.

For ten years he tried to be good but often failed. One day he discovered a missionary chapel just two blocks from the church that had been closed and locked. The missionary told him about Jesus and how to be saved. That very day Luis became a Christian. Later he married a lady who was a school teacher. Today he is the national president of the Holiness Church of Nicaragua.

From an orphan whom no one wanted to the man everyone loves~ all because he prayed to the God who loves the children and wants them to come to Him.

Nicaragua

The Opposing Armies Were Well Armed

Rev. John Dykes

High up in the mountains a little group of Christians regularly met to pray. They were hungry to know God. One day several Bibles were given out in their town. Now they could not only pray but could also study God's Word~ except they did not know where to begin.

They would meet together, place an open Bible on their lap, and ask God to show them where to study. As they quietly waited before God, it seemed the very verses they needed would turn to gold and rise from the pages in front of them. God taught them the plan of salvation. He opened their eyes to the evils of idolatry and led them into baptism. Surely He had answered their prayers in a most amazing way.

Time went on. Despite the civil war raging all around them, the number of believers grew and churches were built. In many ways it was not safe to gather together, but despite the danger people met to worship the God they loved so dearly.

One night as the preacher was preaching, a high-ranking officer of the resistance army came and stood on the platform beside the pulpit. A few minutes later a high ranking officer of the government appeared at the front door. It was a very tense moment~ no one wanted to move. Both opposing army officers were well armed.

Only God could intervene.

The pastor went to the pulpit to try to preach, but he could not. He began to cry, and soon the whole church was weeping. Finally, the pastor asked if anyone wanted to come and get saved. It was very quiet. No one moved until the officer of the resistance group stepped forward, raised his hand and said that he wanted to get saved. He took off his pistol and his dagger and gave them to the preacher. Everyone wondered what would happen next.

The pastor continued giving the invitation, and to their great surprise they heard the firm footsteps of the other officer walking toward the front. You could have heard a pin drop. Finally, he said that he wanted to get saved, too.

He also took off his guns and his daggers and handed them to the preacher. After a very fervent prayer time, the two men stood, hugged each other and asked forgiveness. It was a difficult but very blessed time. Today a faithful pastor and his family continue to minister where war once raged.

Since 1990 Nicaraguans have enjoyed religious freedom~ at least in name.

Mass crusades and evangelism have added many believers to the church.

Amerindians Sumo and Miskito have recently received the New Testament in their language.

 Nicaragua

Pigs, Water and Cows Are Paying the Bills

Rev. Eric Kuhns

Roberto was from the smaller village of Las Delicias (The Delicious) but had come to Tegucigalpa, Honduras, to find work. Life in the city was harder than he thought it would be. Discouraged and ready to quit, God allowed his path to cross the path of missionary Eric Kuhns.

Eric shared the gospel of hope and forgiveness with Roberto. One day Roberto knelt at an altar and gave his whole life~ the good and the bad~ to God. He rose from the altar a new person. He wanted everyone to know about the peace he had found~ including his dad, Jose.

It was not long before Jose came to church and told Eric he had been praying for a missionary to come to his village for 17 years.

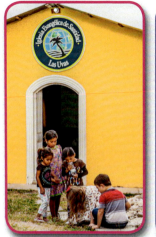

Seventeen years? It had been exactly 17 years since that chapel service in Pennsylvania when Eric had been called to Honduras!

Of course Eric and his family would go. Every week they drove the hour-and-a-half drive to hold services on Jose's front porch. The church grew. Eventually, Jose donated land, and a church was built with Roberto being the new pastor.

In order to support his family Roberto started a pig farm. Shortly afterwards a well was drilled, providing clean safe water for the village. In neighboring Nicaragua God has provided the mission with 200 acres and seven cows. What can you do with seven cows? Sell milk and make cheese! The money which is raised from the farm is providing support for Juan, the faithful national pastor and pays the salary of a church member who tends the farm.

Nicaragua

Costa Rica

"Ticos" and "Ticas"

Soccer is a serious and competitive sport for the Costa Ricans.

Costa Rica has five active volcanoes.

Whoever said frogs don't have class~ especially Mrs. Frog!

Costa Rica was the first Central American country to export coffee. They called it "the grain of gold."

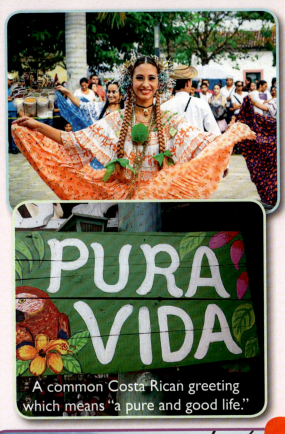

Costa Ricans have a dozen names for rain!

The average rainfall is 100 inches every year.

The rainy season is from May until November.

Be careful! Costa Rica has 20,000 species of spiders!

Zip-lining over the rain forest is a favorite tourist attraction.

PURA VIDA
A common Costa Rican greeting which means "a pure and good life."

Costa Rica is the hummingbird capital of the world.

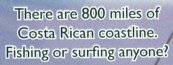

There are 800 miles of Costa Rican coastline. Fishing or surfing anyone?

When you talk about someone you love you say, "You are the other half of my orange."

Going Places!

Taking the gospel to the "ends of the earth" can mean traveling all sorts of ways. Sometimes you will need to climb steep hills or go into deep valleys.

Sometimes you can ride a bike, a motorcycle, or even a donkey.

Sometimes you may need to take a boat, hire a "tuk tuk," or a drive a jeep.

You may even need to ride a "chicken bus," which is sometimes called the "party bus" because of its exciting paint job.

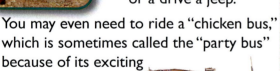

But ALWAYS the mission is to share the GOOD NEWS of the gospel!

Fog on the Mountain
Mrs. Clara West

It was dark and foggy and getting scarier by the minute! My husband and I had traveled this mountain road many times. But tonight we had gotten a late start, and now the fog had rolled in. In desperation we rolled down our windows and stuck our heads outside hoping we could see the road just a little bit better.

We knew for sure, on one side of us was a steep mountain and on the other side was a 5,000 foot drop-off!

We inched along ever so carefully, praying with every turn of the tires that God would keep us in the middle of the narrow road. All of a sudden we noticed a blinking light up ahead. The closer we got to the light, the brighter it blinked. We finally came to the source of the light.

It was a road construction forklift. A construction crew had been working there that day. When everyone else had gone home for the night, one man stayed behind. He knew that anyone driving on the road that night would not have known the road was out and would have driven right over the cliff to certain death below.

One man~ just one~ made a HUGE difference.
Shining your light for Jesus can make a HUGE difference also!

 Costa Rica

Building God's Church in Costa Rica

Mrs. Lynan Redman

Miracles are happening in Costa Rica.

Dale and Lynan Redman are faithfully ministering to both the children and adults in Ngobe-Bugle tribes that just a few years ago was totally shut off from the rest of the world.

Thanks to a work team, a church was built in just FIVE days!

Costa Rican pastors are joining together to develop church planting opportunities.

Catholicism is the official religion, and practicing other faiths could result in trouble.

Ministry to young people is especially important~ two-thirds of Costa Ricans are under age 30.

Short-term mission teams are helping the poor.

Costa Rica

PANAMA

"The Crossroads of the Americas"

Meet the beautiful harpy eagle~ Panama's national bird.

The Panama hat is famous the world over.

The famous Centennial Bridge spanning one of Panama's 500 rivers. It is part of the Pan American Highway.

Panama City is the only city that has a rain forest within its city limits.

Panama is about the size of South Carolina and includes 1,500 islands.

Both soccer and baseball are favorite Panamanian sports.

Iguanas can live up to eight years in the wild.

Panamanians enjoy 1,400 species of orchids.

Welcome to the upside down world of Mr. Three-toed Sloth. He delights in hanging from a tree branch.

There are seven Amerindian tribes living in Panama today.

The Amerindian tribes are known for their beautiful weaving and baskets.

The narrowest point between the Atlantic and Pacific Oceans is found in Panama. It is just 30 miles wide.

Swat That Mosquito!

The warm tropical sun beat down on Pedro's back. It felt good to be out in the sun and working again. He was not doing just any kind of work~ he was helping build the Panama Canal. He remembered a few years ago a group of men had come through his village looking for people to help dig a BIG HUGE ditch between the Atlantic and Pacific Oceans. It had all sounded so exciting~ and now he was the lucky one shoveling dirt on this BIG project. He felt very important.

He was especially happy to be in the sun today, because he and most of his friends were recovering from malaria. Ugh! Malaria- it was awful! Pedro couldn't remember how many days he had laid on the cool cement trying to bring his fever down, but he did know he was horribly miserable. And he was not the only one. The camp nurse told them thousands had gotten sick- over 5,000 had actually died.

Thankfully, those sick days seemed to be behind him. It was rumored he had gotten sick from a mosquito bite. A mosquito bite! How could that be? True, there were lots of mosquitoes everywhere. Those pesky guys made it hard to keep two hands on the shovel, but those tiny creatures could actually make you deathly sick?

Then a new American doctor, William Crawford Gorgas arrived. It seems he had figured out mosquitoes had made a lot of people in Cuba very, very sick. When he and the American troops had cleaned out the stagnant water that was laying in puddles, built toilets, and sprayed chemicals, the Cuban people did not get malaria as much. They really were healthier.

Pedro was so glad Dr. Gorgas had come to their country. Now the canal could be built so much faster with everyone staying much healthier!

Ten years later.

Pedro wasn't shoveling dirt any more. The canal had been completed, and he had a wonderful job as a lock superintendent.

Last Sunday the pastor talked about being thankful. Pedro was grateful for the brave men who had studied hard and figured out what caused malaria. Even at the risk of getting sick themselves, they came to his country and helped so many people stay well.

The Incredible Panama Canal!

The Panama Canal was started in 1903 by France. Flooding, landslides and especially sickness made it a very difficult project.

Over 20,000 laborers died of malaria or yellow fever.

The Americans came in 1904. Dr. William Gorgas is credited with eradicating the mosquito population, thus ridding the canal zone of malaria and yellow fever.

The canal was completed in 1914. It cost $387,000,000.

The Panama Canal is 50 miles long and 10 miles wide.

The canal serves 144 world trade routes.

It takes six to eight hours to go through the canal and cuts 4,000 miles off the trip.

God has given every one of us a talent.
Whatever it is, God can use it!
What do you enjoy doing? What are you good at?
Think about it~ maybe that is YOUR talent.

Panama

"I'll Retire in Heaven"
Mrs. Lynan Redman

"Hurry children! Duck down quick and hide," said Charlotte Teubner to a group of Jewish children she was hiding from the Gestapo. This was not the first group, nor would it be the last. She and her family were involved in a very dangerous mission of rescuing Jewish children who they knew faced certain death.

But not only did the children face death, Charlotte knew if she was caught, she would also be in great danger. Mercifully, the war ended with the lives of many children having been saved. Now it was time for Charlotte to follow God to what He wanted next in her life.

That direction came in the form of a mission organization asking her to go deep into the jungles of Panama to the indigenous Guaymi tribe and translate the Bible into their language.

Charlotte knew in her heart this was the call of God on her life. She never doubted.

When she arrived, her first task was to put the Guaymi language into writing. Then for the next 20 years she worked on translating the Bible and sharing the gospel with her beloved tribe. When she told them of Jesus' power over the evil spirits, they wanted to hear more about this powerful God. Many believed, and many churches were started among the Guaymi people.

Unbeknown to Charlotte, who was living far away from civilization, some of the Jewish children whose lives she had helped save were looking for her. Through some unfortunate circumstances Charlotte had to return home to Germany. Word got out~ Charlotte was back home in Germany!

What a happy reunion Charlotte and the Jewish children (now adults) had! When they heard about her work in Panama, they said, "We are not of your faith, but we want to help you with your mission."

For several years Charlotte received money from her Jewish friends. As she got older, someone asked her when she was going to retire. Her reply was,

"I'll retire in heaven!"

Catholicism is the religion of the majority.
Evangelicals have had a positive reception and are striving to impact their culture.
Every Amerindian group has received the gospel, and most have a New Testament in their language.
The Panamanian church is seeking to reach out to university students.

What Is in Your Hands?

It was neither a fancy university degree nor even a theological degree that was in the hands of Don and Devonna Moore when they and their two daughters, Sheryl and Rochelle went to San Luis in the summer of 1978. Don, having served with the United States Army, was now in the reserves. His interest was in radio. He was a skilled radio technician. Devonna had just completed nurses training and was qualified in maternity related skills.

But God knew those were exactly the skills that were needed high up in a mountain town of San Luis, Honduras. A license had already been received, so Don immediately set about building a radio station~ both the building and the parts. The first antenna was a copper wire strung between two dead pine trees~ but it worked! They were on the air. From that humble beginning transmitters, amplifiers and upgrades were added. God brought qualified staff to help with the broadcasting.

One day a visiting journalist commented that he could not believe such a strong signal was coming from such a small place. Don replied, "Well, the Lord must have taken that small signal and multiplied it many times before it reached the listener." The signal reached the Miskito tribe on the southeastern coast of Honduras. Many became believers as a result.

Because the town of San Luis already had a clinic they requested Faith Missions begin a maternity clinic. Karen Maxey, Karen Fleming and Devonna made up the first team of nurses.

Everyone set to work actually building the clinic~ laying block walls, painting, carpentry, collecting medical supplies. There is a lot which goes into opening a clinic! On May 2, 1979, the doors opened.

Before the day ended the very first new baby had been born in the clinic.

Since then, many improvements and modernization has happened. Over 6,500 babies have been born, including 39 sets of twins and one set of triplets!

The clinic provides round-the-clock services for the community of San Luis. Many patients are cared for in the acute care ward and pediatric room. Treatments and shots, medications and emergency care is provided.

Don reflects, "I thank the Lord that He gave me the call as a young teenager into radio missionary work and led me in the ways to learn the field of electronics."

Central America

"... establish thou the work of our hands upon us; Yea, the work of our hands establish thou it."
Psalm 90:17

So much has happened since the early missionaries went to San Luis. The church has grown and is reaching out and establishing new churches.

Another important development happened under the direction of Daniel and Tiffany Melton. They saw the need for the church to become self-supporting. So they drilled for water and are now selling clean, purified and safe water. A coffee farm was planted and today is producing high quality coffee which is being sold around the world.

Every year a medical team goes to San Luis and outlying villages bringing not only medical help, but also sharing the gospel.

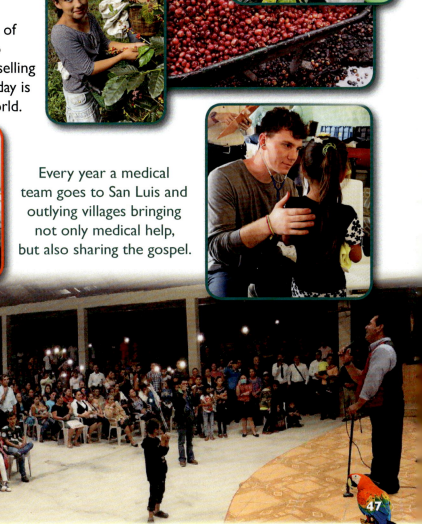

Central America

"Well, kids, I can see you've been busy collecting stories," said Uncle Francisco, as he turned the last page of the stack of papers Juan and Maria had brought to him.

"I've been reading through some of these. All I can say is, **'God sure has been at work in our own Central America! And not just a long time ago either! It's exciting to hear of the many wonderful things that are happening today!'**"

"Some of these stories have really challenged me to think about what I can do for God~ even now while I'm still young," said Juan.

"Yeah, I know what you mean," said Maria. "But I think my favorite discovery was to see how God takes care of His children! Wow! So many of these stories talked about how God watches out for us even when we don't know we're in danger or need help."

"I'm quite sure it doesn't matter where in the world we are, God is taking care of His children," said Uncle Francisco. "Someday I'd like to hear stories from other parts of the world." Juan and Maria agreed~ but for right now they were ready to go ride up to the mission house and visit the "gringos" who had come on a short-term mission team.

Dr. Steve Gibson
Book Visionary

Special thanks to those who contributed. This book could not have happened without you!

Rev. Fausto and Miriam Cebeira, Fundacion Emmanuel
Rev. Brady and Mary Duren, Spanish World Missions
Rev. Sid and Gretel Grant, Hope International Missions
Missionary Juan and Dorcas Gomez, True Gospel Mission
Rev. Steve and Kathy Hight, Evangelistic Faith Missions
Missionary Roger and Damarius Kellogg, Nazarene Missions
Missionary Lydia Hines, Wesleyan Missions
Rev. Eric and Hannah Kuhns, Hope International Missions
Rev. Dale and Lynan Redman, Peace Evangelical Association
Dr. Glen and Helen Reiff, Hope International Missions
Rev. Raymond and Alice Shreve, Evangelical Bible Mission
Rev. Hugh and Kendra Wade, Evangelical Bible Mission
Missionary Clara West, Wesleyan Missions

Joy Budensiek
Author and Complier

Central America

"Before the mountains were brought forth, or ever thou hadst formed the earth and the world, even from everlasting to everlasting, thou art God." Psalm 90:2